For A Better Life

By Henrietta Schleif Pesce

Modern Curriculum Press
Parsippany, New Jersey

Credits

Illustrations: 13: Mapping Specialists

Photos: All photos © Pearson Learning unless otherwise noted.

Front cover: Brown Brothers. Title page: By Courtesy of The Statue of Liberty National Monument. 5, 6: Culver Pictures. 8: By Courtesy of The Statue of Liberty National Monument. 10: Culver Pictures. 11: Archive Photos. 12: Brown Brothers. 14: Culver Pictures. 15: Lewis W. Hine/New York Public Library. 16–17: Brown Brothers. 19: Corbis. 20: Brown Brothers. 22: Culver Pictures. 23: UPI/Corbis/Bettmann. 25, 26: Brown Brothers. 28–29: Archive Photos. 30: Corbis/Bettmann. 33: Brown Brothers. 35: Corbis/Bettmann. 36: Brown Brothers. 38: Corbis/Bettmann. 39: Brown Brothers. 40: Corbis/Bettmann. 41: Culver Pictures. 42: Brown Brothers. 43: By Courtesy of The Statue of Liberty National Monument. 44: National Park Service. 46: *l.* Bob Krist/Corbis; *r.* Gail Mooney/Corbis.

Cover and book design by John Maddalone

Modern Curriculum Press
An imprint of Pearson Learning
299 Jefferson Road, P.O. Box 480
Parsippany, NJ 07054–0480

www.pearsonlearning.com

1-800-321-3106

ISBN 0-7652-2156-X

2 3 4 5 6 7 8 9 10 11   MA   07 06 05 04 03 02 01

Contents

To my immigrant mother,
Molly Fitzgerald Schleif O'Connor—
your spirit has given those you
touch a better life

CHAPTER 1

Ellis Island

This is a story about people. It is a story about men, women, and children from faraway countries. They all had one thing in common. They wanted a better life. They believed they would find it in America. These brave people became immigrants by leaving home and moving to a new country.

The first place these immigrants stepped onto American soil was Ellis Island. This is a small island next to New York City.

Immigrants bound for America from Bulgaria

Everyone in the United States has a connection of some kind to an immigrant. Many Native Americans are believed to have emigrated from Asia to North America thousands of years ago. In the New York area in the 1600s, Native Americans lived on the island of Manhattan and on three smaller islands nearby. These islands came to be known much later as Ellis Island, Liberty Island, and Governor's Island.

Ellis Island

When Dutch immigrants came to America in the 1600s, they bought the islands from the Native Americans. In the 1770s, the islands were sold to a fisherman named Samuel Ellis. He bought the islands because the water around them was filled with fish. Over the years, Samuel Ellis became a rich man from his fishing business.

On July 4, 1794, Samuel Ellis died. He left one of the small islands to his grandson. This island has had many different owners and has been used for many different things since that time. At one point the United States Army built a fort on the island in order to store weapons. At other times the island was used as a hospital and as a prison. It has always been called Ellis Island.

In 1890, almost one hundred years after Samuel Ellis died, President Benjamin Harrison signed a paper naming Ellis Island as an immigration center for the United States. The island was a good place for such a center. It was close to a city where many immigrants came by ship. The immigrants would be taken to the island first. There they would be examined by government officials for diseases and other problems. The officials would then decide whether or not the immigrants could stay in the United States.

Statue of Annie Moore

The immigration center opened on January 1, 1892. On the first day more than 2,000 immigrants landed on the island and were examined. The first immigrant to step onto Ellis Island on that New Year's day was a young girl named Annie Moore. She was from Cork, Ireland. Behind her came her two brothers, Tom and Joe.

Annie's parents had come to America three years earlier. Annie and her brothers had lived with relatives in Ireland until their parents could save enough money so the children could come to America, too.

Annie and her brothers were excited when they arrived at Ellis Island. They were the guests of honor at a ceremony. It celebrated the opening of the new immigration center.

As the first immigrant on Ellis Island, Annie was the star of the ceremony. She was given a ten-dollar gold piece by the Commissioner of Immigration at Ellis Island. Annie and her brothers had never seen a gold piece. Ten dollars was also a great deal of money in 1892.

After the ceremony, Annie, Tom, and Joe were examined to make sure they were in good health. Then their names, ages, and where they were from were registered in the Hall of Records. Finally, the children were told they could stay in the United States. They ran to their parents' waiting arms.

For the next 60 years, people from all over the world came to Ellis Island. The busiest years were from 1892 to 1924. In that time more than 12 million people entered the United States through the Ellis Island immigration center.

One immigrant named Edward Corsi came to America in 1907. He was only 10 years old. He traveled with his mother, stepfather, brother, and two sisters on a steamship crowded with 1,600 other people.

After traveling for 14 days and making it through a terrible storm, the ship sailed into the harbor next to New York City. Edward and his family stood close together on the deck. They looked with wonder at the land of their dreams.

Immigrants crowd the deck of a steamship as it enters New York Harbor.

Immigrants wait to be examined on Ellis Island.

For many immigrants, Ellis Island came to be known as The Isle of Tears. It became a place of sadness for anyone who was turned away because of illness or other problems. They were told they had to go back to where they had come from.

Sometimes families were separated. A father and mother might pass the examination, but they might be told one of their children would not be allowed in because of illness. A mother might find out that her children and husband could stay, but she could not. Then heartbreaking decisions had to be made.

Many people decided to live on Ellis Island for weeks. They waited for a family member to be treated for an illness or examined further. Their sorrow turned to joy if the person was finally told he or she could stay in America.

When he was alive, Samuel Ellis had no idea
how important his tiny island would become. He
never knew his island would be the first place in
America millions of immigrants would see.

A Scandinavian family arrives on Ellis Island.

Ellis Island Notes

From Ellis Island,
the immigrants could see
New Jersey and New York. The New
Jersey shore and the tip of Manhattan
are about a mile across the water.

2
CHAPTER

Dreams of a Better Life

The people who came to Ellis Island were from many different places. They came from small villages and large cities all over the world. At first, most immigrants came from Ireland, Germany, and Scandinavia. Then people from other European countries started to arrive.

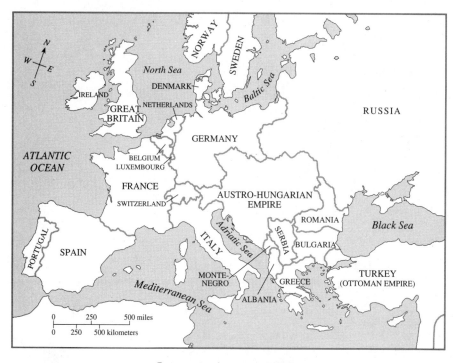

Europe in the early 1900s

Immigrants arriving at Ellis Island

Most of the immigrants who landed on Ellis Island were poor. They had saved for months and years to buy their boat tickets to the United States. They were willing to give up their homes and everything they had.

These people had many reasons to leave their homelands. Some came from countries that were at war. Other people wanted to escape countries where the rulers didn't care if their people were so poor they barely had enough to eat. Still others came because they might be killed in their own countries because of their religious beliefs.

Helen Cohen came from Poland in 1920. She remembered that she was about 10 years old when she decided she had to come to America. Her uncles had already made the journey. She wrote to them that she wanted to be there, too. Finally, Helen Cohen's dream came true. When she first arrived, she said it seemed as though she was in a different world. She described America as peaceful and quiet. For her it was a place where she wasn't afraid to go out at night. She felt free as a bird.

A Russian mother and her children

Immigrants carry their baggage from the boat to the immigration center.

Many immigrants had heard wonderful stories about America. Some people believed that the streets of America were paved with gold. They had heard that all wishes came true in America.

Vartan Hartunian arrived from Turkey in 1922 at age 7. His father had told him that the streets were covered with gold. Vartan found no gold in America, but he still thought it was a heavenly place. It was much better, he said, than the country he had come from where the government made it hard for his family to live freely.

Because so many families who wanted to come to the United States were so poor, family members couldn't all come at once. Often mothers and fathers had to make the difficult decision to leave their children behind with relatives.

Parents journeyed to America to see if their dreams of a better life could come true. Little by little, they would save enough money to send for their children. When the family was finally together in America, their new life could begin.

If both parents could not make the journey, just one member of the family would be sent to America. Usually fathers, uncles, and brothers came first. They worked hard to save enough money to buy boat tickets for the rest of their families. Many families had to wait years before they could all be together again.

Ellis Island Notes

Nearly half of all Americans can trace their ancestry to immigrants who passed through Ellis Island. Did any of your relatives come to America through Ellis Island?

3

CHAPTER

Journey Across the Ocean

For some immigrants, the journey to America was not difficult. They had money and could buy first- or second-class tickets on ships bound for America. First- and second-class passengers had comfortable private cabins with cozy beds and plenty of food.

**First-class passengers are dressed fashionably.
The young woman has a net veil over her face.**

For poor immigrants, the journey to America was not as easy. Most of them had little or no money. The most inexpensive way to travel was by steamship as a steerage passenger. The steamship companies would charge up to $35.00 per adult for steerage passage. Children were half price and babies traveled free. Even so, this was a lot of money for families to spend back then.

For fresh air, immigrants spent as much time as possible outside on the ship's deck.

Families would save for years to raise money. They would borrow from relatives. They even sold their belongings to buy tickets to travel on the ships headed for America.

At times each ship that carried immigrants to America had between 1,500 and 2,000 steerage passengers onboard. People from many different countries were crowded together for weeks in horrible conditions. Their dreams of America were all these immigrants had to help them get through the hardships they faced on the ships.

Steerage passengers were housed in the lowest section of the ship. This section had a few big rooms that were dark, crowded, filthy, and cold. These rooms were only six to eight feet high and had little air. A small washroom had only cold ocean water for washing. The only drinking water was outside on the deck.

The people had little food. By the time the ship had traveled only halfway across the Atlantic Ocean, much of the food was barely fit to eat. Some of it was spoiled, and the rest was soggy. Some immigrants wisely brought their own food rather than depend on anything they might find on the ship. Many people could not eat anyway. They were constantly sick from the swaying motion of the ship as it traveled on the water.

A ship's deck crowded wtih immigrants

Sleeping in the steerage section was almost impossible because so many people were crowded together. The rooms were filled with bunk beds. Immigrants had to sleep with their bags because there was no space to store baggage.

To get some fresh air and light, steerage passengers would try to stay up on deck as much as possible when the weather was good. On the open deck, children played. Adults talked or played music and sang songs.

When the weather turned stormy, the passengers had to go back inside the ship. The ship's crew locked the door that led to the deck. This was so that no one would try to come out and be swept overboard by high waves.

The journey was especially long and hard for the children. It could take up to one month to cross the Atlantic Ocean on a steamship. Boys and girls found ways to entertain themselves. They played games or music. They followed the sailors around as they worked. Some sailors were kind to the children in steerage. They would show them how to tie sailors' knots in the big ropes used on the ship.

Many of the sailors could speak English. This was a new language to many of the children. It was the language of the country they hoped would become their new home. Some sailors would try to teach the children a few words. The children were eager to learn. Later, these words would help them when they reached the United States.

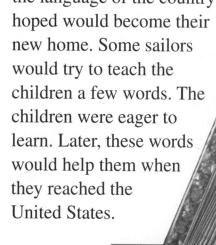

Nathalia and Eugene Gratowics from the Ukraine play music on the ship's deck.

Paul Sturman came to the United States in 1920, when he was 16. He traveled as a steerage passenger from Czechoslovakia. He remembered dancing and music on deck. Someone was always playing a harmonica. He said he made many friends and talked with them endlessly about what America might be like and what they would do after they got there.

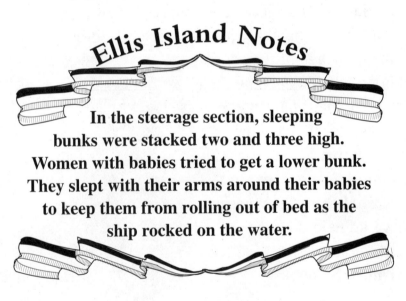

Ellis Island Notes

In the steerage section, sleeping bunks were stacked two and three high. Women with babies tried to get a lower bunk. They slept with their arms around their babies to keep them from rolling out of bed as the ship rocked on the water.

4

CHAPTER

The Beginning

After weeks at sea the ships finally left the rough Atlantic Ocean and entered New York Harbor. As soon as land had been sighted, the immigrants hurried to gather their belongings. They changed into their best clothes. They often wore two or three layers so they would have less to carry. Then the immigrants crowded onto the deck.

New York City from a ship's deck

Everyone's eyes searched in the distance to see this new land. Families would stand close together, holding hands. Their faces turned to catch sight of America. To those who had never seen a large city, the buildings seemed as big as mountains.

Immigrant ships sailed past the Statue of Liberty (bottom center) on their way to Ellis Island (upper left).

A small island loomed in the distance. On this island was a statue of a lady holding a torch high. The Statue of Liberty was the first to welcome these immigrants to their new lives in America. She represented freedom, hope, and opportunity for the millions who looked up at her. She was a sight they would never forget.

Lazarus Salamon recalled the emotions he felt coming to America from Hungary in 1920, at age 16. He described it as suddenly starting a new life among people who spoke a language he didn't understand. He had to forget his childhood and grow up very quickly. Through all his hardships, though, he never lost his hope that life would be better in America. He was right. It was a country where no one was a stranger because all the people were strangers. After all, most Americans had come from someplace else at different times.

Before the passengers could leave the ship, they had to be seen by doctors to be examined for serious diseases they could pass on to other people. First- and second-class passengers were questioned onboard the ship. They were quickly admitted to America if they were found to be healthy.

For steerage passengers it was not as easy. If they passed the doctors' examinations, they were loaded onto a barge and taken to Ellis Island. On the island they would be asked more questions and have to pass more tests.

The immigration center on Ellis Island

When the immigrants got to the island, they sometimes had to wait hours before they could go into the immigration center. They stood without food or water, sometimes in the rain or the hot sun. They worried about what would happen to them.

As they waited, the immigrants had a chance to look at the building they would soon be entering. It was huge. It had enough room for the thousands of people who went through its doors every day. There was a dining room, places for people to sleep, large bathrooms, a hospital, and a laundry room.

There was also a U.S. Post Office and a bank. These were the first U.S. services many immigrants used. In the post office they sent letters to friends or family to tell them that they had arrived in America. At the bank they exchanged the money they had for United States money.

Immigrants used the bank on Ellis Island to exchange money.

As they walked onto Ellis Island, most steerage passengers felt joy and also fear. They were greeted by immigration officers who hurried the immigrants through the front doors of the building and into a large room. This room was called the Baggage Room. It was noisy and crowded. It was also filled with piles and piles of bags from the thousands of people who were coming off the ships.

Some immigrants would not leave their precious belongings. They understood little or no English and carried everything they owned in carryalls and suitcases battered by the long journey. To many, these worn bags contained all they had of the old life. They held prayer books, clothing, photographs, and other family mementos from the old country. Others left their bags among the huge piles already on the floor. They hoped their things would still be there when they returned.

Then the immigrants climbed the steps of a large staircase to what was probably the biggest room they had ever seen. The Great Hall was nearly 171 feet long and 102 feet wide with a 60-foot curved ceiling. It was almost as long as two football fields and as tall as a three-story building. It was filled with a long line of people moving slowly. The new arrivals found a place at the end of the line and began inching their way toward the inspectors.

Celia Adler remembered her first sight of the immigration center. She arrived on Ellis Island from Russia in 1914, at age 12. The only things she had with her were a small basket, a sandwich, and a change of clothes. When she stepped onto the island and saw the center, she was amazed. She had never seen such a big building. Compared with the houses in the town she had left, the center was like a whole city in just one building. To Celia, the center was a beautiful place.

Ellis Island Notes

The largest number of immigrants to arrive on Ellis Island in one day was on April 17, 1906. On that day, 11,745 people entered the immigration center.

Passing Inspection

It was in the Great Hall that the dreaded examination for the steerage passengers began. Almost everyone had heard stories about the nosy and embarrassing questions the inspectors asked. They knew how terrible it was when someone was told they could not stay in the United States.

Immigrants wait in the Great Hall.

To start, doctors examined each immigrant for physical problems. They checked that each child and adult was steady on his or her feet and had a normal appearance. They looked at a person's skin and fingernails and listened for any difficulty breathing. They also examined a person's hair to see if there were any lice or scalp diseases.

The most painful exam was for an eye disease called trachoma. This disease could cause blindness and was contagious. This meant that others could easily catch it if they came in contact with the sick person. If a person had trachoma, he or she would be sent to the island hospital. Immigration records show that this disease kept more than half of all immigrants in the hospital on Ellis Island for a time.

The medical exams helped the inspectors decide if an immigrant was too ill to care for himself or herself in the United States. Each inspection took only a few minutes. If the doctors suspected a problem, they would mark letters on the immigrant's coat with chalk. Some of the letters were X for a mental problem, B for back problems, CT for trachoma, E for a different problem with the eyes, Ft for Feet, and H for heart trouble. Everyone who was marked had to go for further examinations.

After the medical inspection, the immigrants moved on to the next exam. If they were marked, they would not know what it meant until they reached the end of the inspection lines. Any kind of mark filled them with fear. They knew that if one member did not pass the medical inspections, the family could be separated. If people got to the end of the line with no chalk marks on their clothing, they met with the last and most important inspector.

A doctor examines children on Ellis Island.

The last inspector called each immigrant by name to see if the person responded quickly and alertly. Often these names didn't sound anything like the person's real name. Many of the inspectors knew only English. They could not pronounce a foreign name. Sometimes the name had been written incorrectly when the ship left for America. A person might be mistakenly given the name of the city he or she came from. They might be given a name that was easy to pronounce. In this way a person named Skyzertski became Sanders.

The inspector asked every person 29 questions. These included such questions as, "Why have you come to the United States?" "How old are you?" "Do you have any friends or family here?" "What kind of work do you do?" If a person did not speak English, someone would repeat the questions in the immigrant's own language. The person had to answer quickly.

An inspector asks
an immigrant questions.

If the answers were satisfactory, the inspector stamped the immigrant's papers. Then he said, "Welcome to America!" If the inspector didn't like what he heard, he wrote "S.I." on the papers, which meant "Special Inquiry." Then the person had to answer more questions from other inspectors.

After all of the questions were answered, the immigrants went down a staircase that came to be known as the Staircase of Separation. At the bottom, people turned to the right or the left to go to the railroad ticket office or to the ferry to Manhattan. People who had to stay on the island walked straight ahead.

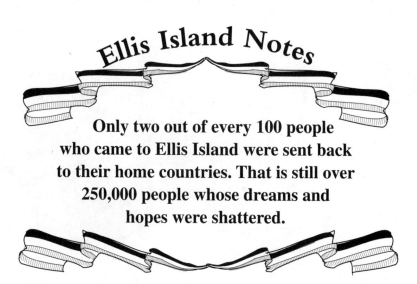

Ellis Island Notes

Only two out of every 100 people who came to Ellis Island were sent back to their home countries. That is still over 250,000 people whose dreams and hopes were shattered.

6 CHAPTER

The Wait

One out of every five people had to stay on Ellis Island for a while. Some of them were marked with chalk for further examinations. Others were waiting for family members who were already in America to come and get them or send them money.

If one family member had to stay on Ellis Island, the whole family waited. Sometimes this wait would take weeks. Then the family had to move into big rooms with many beds, called dormitories.

Dormitories on Ellis Island

Immigrant children have fun on a rooftop playground.

Children and adults who were kept because they were sick stayed in the hospital for one or two weeks until they were better. If people did not get better, they went to a special area of the hospital. There they waited until they could board a steamship to take them back to the country they had come from.

Healthy children who were waiting for family members to be released tried to have fun. There were playgrounds on the roofs of the buildings where they could play. There was even a school where they could begin to learn English. Sometimes performers would come to the island to give shows to entertain the immigrants.

Oreste Teglia came with her family from Italy in 1916, when she was 12. She had to stay on Ellis Island because her sister was sick. Soon, Oreste and her other sister were also sick. She remembered having a temperature and red eyes, which were hurt by the electric lights. She also remembered getting oatmeal with brown sugar on it for breakfast. Because she had never seen oatmeal before, she wouldn't eat it. So she put the oatmeal on the windowsill for the birds to eat.

Immigrant children sitting on a window ledge

Milk is poured for children on Ellis Island.

Some immigrants remembered ordinary things that happened during the weeks they spent on Ellis Island when they were children. Donald Roberts came from Wales in 1925, when he was 12. He remembered that a man came around every morning and every afternoon with a steel cart. In the cart was warm milk for the children. The man would blow a whistle or ring a bell, and all the children would get in line. He used a huge metal pitcher to pour milk into small paper cups. He gave every child a cup.

When at last the wait was over, people got a stamped card that said they could enter the United States. They rushed to leave Ellis Island. Some people were met by relatives. Others went alone into their new country.

A family is ready to enter the United States.

Ellis Island Notes

Immigrants who tried to buy ferry or railroad tickets had to be careful if they didn't speak English. Some people tried to trick them by taking their money and giving them nothing.

7

CHAPTER

Welcome to a New Home

The immigrants whose relatives came to Ellis Island to meet them had cheerful reunions or meetings right on the island. Many children met fathers they hadn't seen for years and whom they didn't recognize. Their fathers had come to America years before to earn the money to bring the rest of the family over.

Immigrants from Guadalupe wait for their relatives.

Katharine Beychok came from Russia in 1910 at the age of 10. She remembered meeting her father, who had left to go to America when she was two years old. She didn't know what her father looked like. When a man came toward her, she thought he looked familiar. He was tall and thin, with brown, wavy hair. She realized later that she knew this man was her father because he looked exactly like her.

At the train station or the ferry dock, there was a lot of excitement and confusion. Ann Vida was only 10 when she came from Hungary in 1921. Ann remembered people who were there to help her family understand where to go and what to do. Everyone wore tags identifying where they should go. People could direct the immigrants even if they could not speak their language. These people were best remembered for telling the immigrants that everything would soon be all right.

A young girl is ready to leave Ellis Island.

Over the years, thousands of men, women, and children from all over the world came to Ellis Island. Most of them passed inspection and stayed in America. Finally, so many immigrants had traveled to America that the United States changed its immigration laws. The country didn't want so many newcomers. Fewer immigrants were allowed to come in.

Gradually, Ellis Island stopped being used as a federal immigration station. Officials tried to find other uses for the huge building. Nothing seemed to work. In 1954, Ellis Island was officially closed.

The island sat abandoned for over 10 years. It became overgrown with weeds. The buildings started to decay. People began to notice that a piece of history was being lost. They wanted to take care of the island. It was important to the many immigrants and their families who had come through there.

In 1965 the U.S. government put the National Park Service in charge of Ellis Island. The National Park Service raised money to restore, or fix, the buildings. They wanted to turn the island into an immigration museum.

During this time, people could visit Ellis Island and tour the old buildings. They saw the Great Hall, the inspectors' station, and even the chalk left by the inspectors.

The Great Hall before and after restoration

A huge rebuilding project was started. After many years the National Park Service opened a restored Ellis Island to the public in 1990. Many people wanted to visit the immigration museum that honored people who went through so much to come to the United States.

Today you can visit the museum and experience firsthand what it was like to be an immigrant on Ellis Island. You can walk into the Baggage Room and climb the stairs to the Great Hall. You can go through the inspection stations. There are exhibits, movies, and photographs.

There is also an Oral History Project based at the Ellis Island Museum. In their own words, over 1,500 immigrants have had a chance to tell their amazing stories. These are stories about people who left their homes for a better life in America.

Ellis Island Notes

Visitors to Ellis Island can enter a name in a computer to find information about immigrants and their own ancestors who came to the island.

Glossary

conditions [kun DIHSH unz] ways certain people, things, or places are

contagious [kun TAY jus] spread by contact with other people, such as a disease

dormitories [DOR muh tor eez] large rooms with beds for a number of people

harbor [HAHR bur] a place where ships can stay, load and unload cargo, and be safe from storms and rough water

immigrants [IHM uh grunts] people who come to a new country to make a new home

inspectors [ihn SPEK turz] people who examine or review something such as people, buildings, or printed papers

museum [myoo ZEE um] a building or room for keeping and showing objects that are important in history, art, or science

reunions [ree YOON yunz] gatherings of people who have been apart

steerage [STEER ihj] in earlier times, the part of a ship for passengers paying the lowest price for tickets

trachoma [truh KOH muh] a disease of the inner part of the eyelid and the surface of the eyeball